| | | DATE DUE | |
|---|---|---|---|
| | | | |
| | | | |
| | | | |
| | | | |
| | | | |
| | | | |
| | | | |
| | | | |
| | | | |
| | | | |
| | | | |
| | | | |
| | | | |

By
Hayley Mitchell Haugen

**KIDHAVEN PRESS**
*An imprint of Thomson Gale, a part of The Thomson Corporation*

THOMSON
——★——™
GALE

Detroit • New York • San Francisco • New Haven, Conn. • Waterville, Maine • London

THOMSON
——————*——————™
GALE

Cover photo: Gargoyles on the balustrade of the Grande Galerie, replica of a 12th century original (stone), Viollet-le-Duc, Eugene Emmanuel (1814-79)/Notre Dame, Paris, France, Lauros/Giraudon/The Bridgeman Art Library International; © Walter S. Arnold, www.stonecarver. com, 14-15, 22; Associated Press, 39; Joseph H. Bailey/National Geographic/Getty Images, 7; © Oliver Bogler/iStockphotos.com, 18; © John Butchofsky-Houser/CORBIS, 26 (main photo); Corel, 19; © David Crausby/Alamy, 5; © Vicki Fisher/Alamy, 33; © fotofacade. com/Alamy, 12; © JLF Capture/ Judy Foldetta/iStockphotos.com, 34; John Jameson/Princeton University Office of Communications, 25; © jolley_limey/Mark Jessup/iStockphoto.com, 26 (inset); © eddie linssen/Alamy, 30; © Ludovic Maisant/CORBIS, 8 (main photo); Mary Evans Picture Library, 27; © Oxford Picture Library/Alamy, 8 (inset); Graeme Norways/Stone/Getty Images, 13; PhotoDisc, 10; © Adrian Sherratt/Alamy, 21; Peter Sís, HarperCollins Children's Books, 37; © David Toccafondi, 11 (both photos) © Michael Westhoff/ iStockphoto.com, 31.

*For more information, contact*
KidHaven Press
27500 Drake Rd.
Farmington Hills, MI 48331-3535
Or you can visit our Internet site at http://www.gale.com

---

**LIBRARY OF CONGRESS CATALOGING-IN-PUBLICATION DATA**

Haugen, Hayley Mitchell, 1968–
Gargoyles / by Hayley Mitchell Haugen.
    p. cm. — (Monsters)
Includes bibliographical references and index.
ISBN-13: 978-0-7377-3627-4 (hard cover : alk. paper)
ISBN-10: 0-7377-3627-5 (hard cover : alk. paper)
1. Gargoyles in art—Juvenile literature. I. Title. II. Series: Monsters (KidHaven Press)
NX650.G38H38 2006
729'.5—dc22

                                                            2006007124

---

Printed in the United States of America

# CONTENTS

# Chapter 1

# The Gargoyles Are Watching!

High above the streets of the city of Den Bosch in the Netherlands, a terrifying winged creature lunges out from the side of the Cathedral of Saint John. It grimaces at a group of stone-carved humans who have scaled the cathedral to straddle the **flying buttresses**, and they recoil from it in horror. Across the ocean in America, a wide array of menacing-looking **griffins**, creatures that are half eagle and half lion, bare their fangs and grip the rooftops of the Washington National Cathedral with their sharp talons. On the same cathedral, a scary devil with a pitchfork, horns, and a pointed tail tries to tempt passersby to taste from his basket of forbidden fruit.

Have the world's cathedrals been overtaken by monsters? Yes, there are **gargoyles** among us! But there is no cause for alarm. Humans and gargoyles have lived together for thousands of years.

## A HISTORY IN STONE

The monsters called gargoyles are various kinds of creatures sculpted from stone. They perch on the outer edges of buildings around the world. The history of gargoyles goes back many thousands of years

*The frightening faces of gargoyles glare down from many city buildings and cathedrals.*

to ancient Egyptian, Greek, and Roman architecture. But most of these beasts were carved from limestone or marble between A.D. 900 and 1500. During this period, known as the Middle Ages, people were more superstitious than they are today. They believed that demons walked among them on earth, so many of their stone carvings depicted these fiends.

While gargoyles originally represented the fantastic beasts of human imagination, they also served a specific purpose. They were created as waterspouts. Their purpose was to push rainwater away from the walls of medieval buildings. In fact, the English word gargoyle comes from the old French word *gargouille*, meaning "gullet" or "throat." This refers to the gargoyle's drainlike function.

## Gargoyles and Grotesques

Just because they serve a practical purpose does not mean that gargoyles are any less scary as monsters. Most gargoyles are placed high up on buildings. They may be fifty floors or more above street level. So, stone carvers exaggerated their features so that they could be seen by people walking far below them. Thus, gargoyles often have wide, open mouths, displaying sharp fangs or long, protruding tongues. Their eyes frequently bulge from their sockets as they watch people in the streets. Their ears are usually sharp and pointed. If they have wings, they are often spread wide. They look as

*Water spews from the mouth of a gargoyle, which acts as a spout to divert rainwater from the building.*

though they could lurch from the ledges where they have been captured in stone and glide through the world of humans.

Some gargoyle-like carvings do not serve as waterspouts. The griffins on the Washington National Cathedral are one example of these. They are usually referred to as **grotesques**. Things that are grotesque are usually thought to be bizarre, ugly, and frightening. As their name suggests, grotesques are often as monstrous as gargoyles.

Unlike gargoyles, grotesques, such as this griffin (above) and monstrous face (right), do not serve as waterspouts.

Other examples of grotesques are found on San Francisco's Grace Cathedral. This cathedral is home to the tallest **Gothic**-style spire in the United States. Rising 117 feet (about 36m) above the rooftop, the spire is encircled by eight two-legged, winged dragons. These **wyverns** stretch more than 4 feet (1.2m) out from the side of the spire. Their wings are tight at their sides, ready for flight.

The **quad** at the University of Pennsylvania also contains more than 450 different grotesques. Some of these figures appear to be friendly. Others could give people nightmares. These figures include a devilish-looking jester, a **cherub** in the clutches of a threatening monkey-lizard, and a blind man petting the ghoulish head of a skeleton.

Although they do not have water pipes in their mouths as true gargoyles do, grotesques serve a similar purpose. Water bounces off their heads and tails and other features instead of pounding directly against the structure's walls. Today, people usually refer to all fantastically carved creatures on buildings as gargoyles.

## THE MANY FACES OF GARGOYLES

Whether clinging to the walls of university buildings, lunging from the ledges of skyscrapers, or scaling the spires and flying buttresses of Gothic cathedrals, gargoyles come in many different forms. Some gargoyles combine the traits of two or more different animals—like the griffins on the

Washington National Cathedral. These beasts are known as **chimeras.** The creature that is specifically named the chimera is actually a combination of a goat, a lion, and a serpent. But other figures are also regarded as chimeras. These include sphinxes, which combine a human head with a lion's body, and centaurs, which are half man and half horse.

## IN MOTION

Whatever their form, gargoyles are also almost always depicted in motion. A group of at least five frightening beasts seem to slide single file down a buttress at the Henry VII Chapel at Westminster Abbey in London, for example. Some other beasts even seem to be eating the structures on which they perch. Their mouths chomp on column tops or bases.

Nearby in Kent, England, for example, a gleeful, sharp-toothed monster chomps on a column at Canterbury Cathedral. At Barfreston Cathedral,

*Chimeras, such as this goatlike beast, combine traits from several creatures.*

*Two jesters (above) and a blind man holding a skull are among more than 450 grotesques on the University of Pennsylvania campus.*

also in Kent, a group of eight creatures crunch their way through the columns separating the panels of a rose window. Rose windows are the round decorative windows that are a common feature in Gothic cathedrals. It is an unusual treat, however, to see one being eaten by gargoyles!

Other gargoyles become animated by the way they clutch at their throats as if ready to vomit. During rainstorms, they do, indeed, look as though they

The Gargoyles Are Watching!

*During rainstorms, a gargoyle clutching its throat spews rainwater onto those walking below.*

are "losing their lunch" on unlucky passersby. Sometimes a gargoyle might clutch another creature in its arms or mouth. And that creature seems to drool, spit, or vomit on those below. At the Cathedral of Santa Maria in Milan, Italy, for example, a man stands with the weight of a lion hefted onto his shoulders. When it rains, the water pours from the lion's open mouth.

Gargoyles

# GARGOYLES, GARGOYLES EVERYWHERE!

While few of the gargoyles carved during the Middle Ages exist in their original form today, gargoyles are easy to spot. The buildings of New York City, for example, are home to the largest gathering of gargoyles in America. With eighteen cathedrals—more than any other city in the world—it is no wonder gargoyles have found comfortable homes there.

*This steel gargoyle is a celebrated feature of New York City's Chrysler Building.*

The New York Stock Exchange on Wall Street is housed in the famous Woolworth Building. Constructed in 1913, this building was the world's tallest until the Empire State Building was erected in 1930. The Woolworth Building was the world's first skyscraper built in the Gothic style. Many of its gargoyles are at street level. But high above the city, caught forever in the act of flight, 26 dragons leap overhead from the 49th and 51st floors.

Another famous American venue for gargoyles is the Washington National Cathedral in Washington, D.C. Lining the roof of that building, which overlooks both the Capitol and the White House, are 112 gargoyles. What is remarkable about this is that no two of them are alike.

The figures include devils, dragons, serpents, frogs, bats, and other tortured souls. Private donations, not state or federal funds, paid for most of these gargoyles. Through a donations program that ran for about twenty years starting in the 1960s, people paid eighteen hundred dollars to add a gargoyle to the rooftop.

These gargoyles usually have personal meaning for those donating them. A dentist, for example,

*A wide variety of creatures adorns the Washington National Cathedral, such as these grotesques awaiting installation.*

paid for the figure of a man polishing a rhino's tooth. The former manager of the cathedral bookstore is honored by an elephant carrying a book in its trunk. Many of the cathedral's gargoyles are more whimsical than frightening. But more tradition-ally monstrous figures can be found there as well.

In one area of the Washington National Cathe-dral, a fierce wild boar with long tusks seems to spring right out of the structure at onlookers. Else-where, a half-human, half-beast sits with its fingers shoved in its ears. This creature is said to represent the forces of evil refusing to listen to the Christian sermons given inside the church. Another gargoyle with a threatening message is the one depicting the skeleton of a bird, or some other winged creature, entangled by a snake. The snake tauntingly pokes its head out from the poor animal's eye socket. It has been said that this gargoyle shows humankind's awareness that demon forces are forever present. Indeed, this gargoyle looks like it is waiting for a chance to devour those around it.

Whether they are true gargoyles or grotesques, the monsters people refer to as gargoyles have a firm grip on the human imagination. Through myth and legend, gargoyles have come alive, springing from the shadowy corners of cathedrals and into their roles as protector or fiend.

Gargoyles

# CHAPTER 2

# WHEN GARGOYLES TAKE FLIGHT

**P**erched upon public buildings, grimacing or smiling at all who pass by below, gargoyles awaken the public's senses. The little hairs on people's arms raise with the creepy sensation that they are being watched or followed by something horrific above. Or chuckles rise in people's throats when they spy a naughty gargoyle in the rain, spitting water on passersby. The senses are kept alert by the everyday presence of gargoyles. It is in the imagination, however, that gargoyles truly take flight. They come alive through the myths and legends that have been passed down through the centuries.

*Perched high on a building, this gargoyle appears ready to leap from its ledge.*

## GARGOYLES WITH HEARTS OF GOLD

Despite their often fearsome appearance, some legends describe gargoyles as friendly creatures. In these legends, they are said to protect those who live near the buildings they nest on. By looking grotesque and repulsive, these well-meaning gargoyles stand guard to frighten off evil spirits. At night, they are said to come alive. They glide through the darkness on outstretched wings. Or they patrol the streets, their claws clicking across cobblestones, keeping watch while the townsfolk sleep.

Michael D. Lampen is the archivist at Grace Cathedral. He describes the cathedral's eight wyverns as performing a protective role. "One can think of them as sort of 'holy pit bulls,' whose job is to dispel the evil forces, lightning, plague, war, and other calamities that may threaten the city,"[1] he says.

Although Grace Cathedral's two-legged dragons are mythological beasts, realistic animals are also celebrated for their ability to protect. As the

*The lion, which often appears on public buildings, is a symbol of courage and strength.*

king of beasts, for example, the lion is one of the most frequently carved figures on public buildings. The lion has long been a symbol of courage and strength. One such beast stands outside the New York State Capitol building in Albany. It is a majestic and ferocious-looking carved lion. To all who see it, that wide-eyed, roaring beast clearly looks like it is protecting those within.

The figure of the Green Man is another protective gargoyle commonly found on Gothic buildings. The Green Man is usually shown as the face of a man surrounded by a wreath of tree branches, fruit, or flowers. Sometimes he also has leaves spilling from his mouth.

## POWERFUL SYMBOLS

To the early Celtic peoples of Ireland and Scotland, the Green Man was seen as a symbol of **fertility** and rebirth. As **pagans**, the Celts believed in numerous gods who lived among them as part of the natural landscape. Trees were especially sacred to the Celts, and the figure of the Green Man helped them celebrate their environment.

Each spring, the Celts held a festival in celebration of trees and the new season of natural growth. During this May Day celebration, they danced around a sacred tree and gave thanks to the Green Man. Later, when the Green Man figure began to be carved into the churches, the partygoers danced around the church as well.

*The early Celtic peoples of Ireland and Scotland believed that the Green Man figure (pictured) represented fertility and rebirth.*

The same Celts who praised the protective figure of the Green Man also believed in a more gruesome good-luck charm. Celtic myth says that bringing home the severed head of one's enemy can both ward off evil and bring good luck. After severing an enemy's head in battle, Celts are said to have mounted it on a stick outside their home. Some hung heads directly on buildings. Severed heads tend to rot and get stinky pretty quickly. It is not surprising, then, that stone representations of severed heads would have been more appealing!

Medieval clergymen understood the Celts' beliefs. They used that knowledge to convert them to Christianity. They had the friendly looking Green Man and the more terrible-looking severed heads carved on their churches. These figures made the buildings more inviting to the Celts. As in Celtic beliefs, the severed heads served as symbols of luck and protection. The clergy then made use of other carvings within the church to illustrate their teachings.

In this sense, some gargoyles are said to have served as scripture in stone. They preached the

*This mischievous-looking pig is an example of a gargoyle that does not serve a religious purpose.*

Gospel of the church through the stories they enacted. Today, gargoyles still tell stories, but not always to spread a religious message. One such gargoyle is a weeping sea turtle, which was donated to the Washington National Cathedral in 1976. It honors the life of an environmentalist who fought for the protection of giant turtles. The weeping turtle will continue to keep the activist's political message alive long after his death.

Another example of a gargoyle that does not serve a religious purpose is the figure of a cat on the Cathedral of Saint John the Divine in New York City. Like any housecat, this kitty is curled up in a ball with its tail in its mouth. But this common scene from American households has a deeper meaning. As author Suzanne Haldane explains, "The cat is considered independent, quiet, passive—and sometimes lazy. Making himself into a complete circle by biting his own tail, this cat symbolizes eternal laziness."[2]

## ENTERTAINERS

Yet another idea about gargoyles is that they once served as a kind of medieval entertainment. They were simply there to amuse people. This explains some of the more lighthearted gargoyles in existence. One such gargoyle is the laughing winged dog on the National Bank of Belgium in Leuven, Belgium. Another is the camera-toting monkey that appears to be taking pictures of students as they rush to classes at Princeton University in New Jersey.

## WHERE THERE IS GOOD, THERE IS ALSO EVIL

While some gargoyles are whimsical, others give off an image of menace. Those with glaring, bulging eyes and grimacing, twisted mouths surely do not have friendly intentions. These gargoyles seem to match the legends that say gargoyles are the souls of condemned sinners. They have been frozen in stone on their way to the underworld. They will remain forever locked outside church, with no means of gaining forgiveness. Other scholars argue that these fearsome figures serve as a warning. They warn that evil lurks outside the church and that safety can be found within.

Scholars may argue about why gargoyles look so fearsome, but there is no arguing with the fact that some are downright scary. Some gargoyles, for example, pull their mouths open impossibly wide with their hands. This creates a more frightful expression. They even stick out their tongues, on occasion, to mock people below. These mouth-pullers, as they are called, are often regarded as giants. They are frequently found in medieval art.

With their open mouths, gargoyle giants are taunting. They remind all who pass by that they could easily be devoured as an afternoon snack. This warning is taken one step further at Saint John the Divine, the largest cathedral in the world. Here,

*Observant students at Princeton University may notice this monkey with a camera perched atop a campus building.*

*These mouth-puller gargoyles, with their exaggerated expressions, can be seen from below by passersby.*

a giant is portrayed actually swallowing a man whole! The poor man's legs forever hang from the giant's mouth like two strands of spaghetti about to be slurped in.

## THE LEGEND OF *LA GARGOUILLE*

By far the most well-known and often-repeated legend about gargoyles is the story of the ferocious water dragon named *La Gargouille*. The fierce beast lived in the River Seine near Paris, France, and terrorized the nearby village of Rouen. He gobbled up ships and sailors. He set buildings aflame with his breath of fire. He caused floods when he spouted water from the river over the village. And although the dragon constantly demanded human sacrifices, he could never be appeased. His reign of terror continued.

Then, the legend says, sometime between the years 520 and 600, a priest arrived in the village. The priest, Saint Romanus, pledged to the townspeople that he would subdue the dragon and free

*According to ancient legend, a fierce beast called* La Gargouille *(pictured) terrorized French villagers until tamed by Saint Romanus.*

the village from its terror forever. In return, he asked that the people help him build a church and become his congregation. The villagers agreed, but none thought Saint Romanus would succeed in his quest.

Much to their surprise, Saint Romanus defeated the terrible dragon. He did so by simply making the sign of the cross above the beast. The creature was tamed. Saint Romanus led it through the village, like a dog, on a leash made from his own priest's robe. In jubilation over the dragon's defeat, the villagers set the beast ablaze after the battle. Its body was destroyed, but its head and neck would not burn because they were used to the intense heat of the monster's own breath. So the people mounted these remains on their new church. It served as a reminder of Christian victory over evil. Later, a dragon was carved on the cathedral itself. It remains there today—some say, as the very first gargoyle.

Gargoyles

# Chapter 3

# Inspired by Gargoyles

Gargoyle myths and legends have survived for hundreds of years. The influence of these tales and musings continues to inspire merchandisers, writers, and artists today.

## Gargoyles for Sale! Get Your Gargoyles!

Gargoyle merchandise abounds in popular American culture. Gargoyles can be found in local gardening stores, mail-order catalogs, and on the Internet auction site eBay. In July 2006 alone, eBay listed more than 300 gargoyle-related items for sale. That month, for $525, eBay shoppers could

*Gruesome gargoyle heads crowd a shop window display.*

purchase a pair of unique wall-mounted gargoyle candlestick holders. And for just $16.99, more frugal shoppers could purchase an 8-inch (20cm) stone gargoyle in the shape of a winged dog. Whether they shop on eBay or not, gargoyle enthusiasts have no problem expanding their collections. Gargoyles and gargoyle images have become popular gifts as lawn ornaments, bookends, blankets, jewelry, and more.

Ed Clancy is the owner of the Dedo Gargoyle Company in Edgewater, New Jersey. He was so enthusiastic about one cute, friendly looking gargoyle his company makes that he couldn't resist making up his own myth about the little creature. According to his story, the gargoyle, named Dedo, was the creation of a medieval nun. The nun was terrified by the grotesque gargoyles lurching from the shadows at Notre Dame Cathedral in Paris.

To help make herself feel more at ease in the cathedral, the nun formed Dedo from clay. She then placed him high atop the cathedral, where no one would be likely to find him. There the squat little Dedo sat, quietly hugging his knees, undisturbed for centuries. And Dedo would have remained hidden,

*Many people display gargoyle statues as ornamental figures in their gardens.*

the legend goes, had it not been for a young boy who got lost in the cathedral one night. Suddenly the little boy slipped. He would have fallen to his death had it not been for Dedo, who caught him in his friendly arms. Thus, Dedo became known as a symbol of protection, a tiny fighter of evil at Notre Dame.

The more Clancy sold his gargoyle through his Web site and mail-order catalogs, the more the legend of Dedo began to spread. Gargoyle fans who were interested in learning more about the little fellow ultimately contacted Notre Dame for more information. It was then that they learned that the legend did not originate in Paris. Eventually, the story was traced back to Clancy, and he admitted that he had made it up himself to help make his gargoyle more interesting to potential buyers. People have shown so much interest in the story, however, that Clancy plans to write a children's book about Dedo. He might even turn his story into a movie someday.

## HAUNTED FACES

The legend of Dedo proves that even a salesman can be inspired to write about gargoyles. So it is not surprising that other creative minds have found inspiration in them as well. Stephen King, for example, is America's most famous writer of horror novels. In 1987, King was asked to write the introduction for a book of photographs of gargoyles in

*Horror novelist Stephen King once referred to gargoyles as "nightmares in the sky."*

America. Although he is a famous writer, King was nervous about accepting the project at first. He admits that he did not know anything about gargoyles at the time.

After he studied the photographs and later explored the gargoyles of New York City for himself, King was inspired to write his essay. He described the figures as "nightmares in the sky."[3] This later became the title for the book of photographs. As a horror writer, King appreciated the way the gargoyles he studied gave him the creeps. To him, they

Inspired by Gargoyles

felt alive. "They may not actually fly off the buildings they adorn," King wrote, "or hide behind their soot-blackened towers and chimneys when those aware of their presence pass below, but they are, nonetheless, alive."[4] In particular, King was attracted to the gargoyles' faces. They are, he said, "faces which will haunt you when the lights are out."[5]

## Beastly Cartoon Characters

Greg Weisman is another writer who has found inspiration in gargoyles. He fondly recalls the gargoyles of Oxford University in England, where he attended school. These gargoyles later helped inspire him to create the animated television series *Gargoyles* for the Walt Disney Company.

In this series, the gargoyles are an extremely powerful race of winged beasts. Cast in stone as

*A grimacing gargoyle appears ready to pounce on those below.*

part of a curse, they cannot move during the day. At night, their marble turns to flesh and they glide through the air, protecting their lair. The gargoyle race is betrayed by a human, however. Only seven of the creatures survive through the centuries and into the 1990s. Once their curse is broken, they no longer return to stone each day. Instead, they battle good and evil and must learn to trust and be trusted by humans in the modern world.

These beastly characters were an immediate hit with viewers when the series first aired in 1994. The show ran for three seasons, totaling 65 episodes. It was taken off the air in 1997. Gargoyle action figures and fan clubs emerged from the hit show and are still popular today with fans. Some fans are so interested in the *Gargoyles* series that hundreds of them attend the *Gargoyles* convention each year. The convention has been held in such cities as New York; Williamsburg, Virginia; and Dallas, Texas. In June 2006, more than 350 fans met in Valencia, California, to celebrate the tenth anniversary of the convention.

## CREEPY POEMS

The *Gargoyles* animated series is most appropriate for teen viewers. But younger children are often attracted to monsters like gargoyles as well. With this in mind, author Jack Prelutsky teamed up with illustrator Peter Sís to create a book of illustrated monster poems called *The Gargoyle on the Roof.* In this book, a mother gargoyle sings her babies a midday lullaby, wishing them "lovely daymares." She also promises them that when the "moon and stars return," they will be allowed to "soar throughout the night."[6] In their own poem to their mother, the same gargoyle babies beg to stay up extra late. They want to make mischief by plunging through the sky toward frightened passersby below.

In the poem "The Gargoyle on the Roof," a creepy, bug-eyed creature vows to protect his building from those who wish it harm. He warns that his "fiery red" eyes are watching. His deadly claws are ready to protect his lair. And his ears can "hear your footfalls from a thousand miles away."[7] In these poems and drawings, the gargoyles are both frightening and lovable.

## Stone Carvers

Today's stone carvers help keep people's fearful yet loving relationship with gargoyles alive. They do so by continuing to practice their art. When necessary, these artisans repair the world's oldest and most famous gargoyles. Many have been damaged by hundreds of years of stormy weather. Others have been hurt by industrial pollution and by chemical pollutants released by cars.

Gargoyle sculptors also create new gargoyles. And they still use the same tools used long ago: the hammer and chisel. In fact, the only new tool to come into the trade since medieval times is the

*Jack Prelutsky's book* The Gargoyle on the Roof *is filled with poems about both frightening and lovable gargoyles.*

pneumatic chisel. This motor-driven device is a kind of air hammer. It helps carvers chisel out the details on their gargoyles more quickly.

## CREATING GARGOYLES

Whatever tools are used, it takes years of practice to become a master carver. In her book *American Gargoyles,* Darlene Trew Crist writes about Vincenzo Palumbo, a fifth-generation stone carver. Palumbo worked with his father on the gargoyles of the Washington National Cathedral. He is now the master carver there. He says that carvers learn to judge each other's work just by listening to the artisans at work. Crist explains, "The sound made when a chisel hits stone is enough for trained ears to know when a mistake has been made and also to recognize when a carving will be a masterpiece."[8]

Sometimes the creatures stone carvers create seem to stretch high into the clouds. However high they climb, these works still often reflect upon the popular culture far below. In the 1980s, for instance, sculptor Jay Hall Carpenter and stone carver Patrick J. Plunket created the fierce figure of Darth Vader for the northwest tower of the Washington National Cathedral. The evil villain is from George Lucas's science-fiction film series *Star Wars*. It was suggested by Christopher Rader of Kearney, Nebraska, when he took part in a competition to design a gargoyle for the cathedral as a child. His sketch won third place in the competition. But his

*A sculptor carefully transforms a block of stone into a monstrous and memorable gargoyle.*

gargoyle best captures the original grotesque and ferocious characteristics of gargoyles of medieval lore. Other winning contributions included a raccoon, a little girl wearing pigtails and braces, and a large-toothed, umbrella-carrying man. Rader's Darth Vader, however, reminds sightseers that, at heart, gargoyles are monsters!

# NOTES

## CHAPTER 2: WHEN GARGOYLES TAKE FLIGHT

1. Quoted in Darlene Trew Crist, *American Gargoyles: Spirits in Stone.* New York: Clarkson Potter, 2001, p. 40.
2. Suzanne Haldane, *Faces on Places: About Gargoyles and Other Stone Creatures.* New York: Viking, 1980, p. 32.

## CHAPTER 3: INSPIRED BY GARGOYLES

3. Stephen King, *Nightmares in the Sky: Gargoyles and Grotesques.* New York: Viking, 1998, p. 19.
4. King, *Nightmares in the Sky,* p. 25.
5. King, *Nightmares in the Sky,* p. 35.
6. Jack Prelutsky, *The Gargoyle on the Roof.* New York: Greenwillow, 2006, p. 11.
7. Prelutsky, *The Gargoyle on the Roof,* p. 40.
8. Crist, *American Gargoyles,* p. 94.

# GLOSSARY

**cherub:** A small angel, usually portrayed as a child with chubby, rosy cheeks.

**chimeras:** Beasts made up of the characteristics of two or more animals.

**fertility:** The condition of being able to produce offspring.

**flying buttresses:** Architectural supports often found on Gothic cathedrals.

**gargoyles:** The various kinds of creatures sculpted from stone that perch on buildings throughout the world. Traditionally, they are used as waterspouts, to direct rainwater away from a building's walls.

**Gothic:** An architectural style prevalent in western Europe from the twelfth through the fifteenth centuries and characterized by pointed arches and rib vaulting, which emphasized the impression of height.

**griffins:** Beasts that are half lion and half eagle.

**grotesques:** Bizarre, ugly, or frightening figures found on buildings that do not serve as waterspouts as traditional gargoyles do.

**pagans:** Follwers of a religion that worship more than one god.

**quad:** A square, usually grassy area on a university campus through which much foot traffic passes.

**wyverns:** Two-legged, winged dragons of medieval legend.

# For Further Exploration

## Fiction

Eve Bunting, *Night of the Gargoyles.* New York: Clarion, 1999. This popular story with charcoal illustrations describes    both the funny and creepy antics of gargoyles who descend from their museum perches to frighten a watchman at night.

Debbie Dadey and Marcia Thornton Jones, *Gargoyles Don't Drive School Buses.* New York: Scholastic, 1996. In this book from the Adventures of the Bailey School Kids series, the kids wonder if their bus driver, Mr. Stone, could be a real life gargoyle. He looks like one, and one of the gargoyles from atop the old city library is missing!

Dav Pilkey, God Bless the Gargoyles. Orlando, FL: Harcourt Children's Books, 1999. This rhyming tale tells the story of lonely gargoyles who are befriended by angels who travel with them through the city at night.

Jack Prelutsky *The Gargoyle on the Roof.* New York: Greenwillow, 2006. This illustrated book offers fun and spooky rhyming poems about gargoyles,

43

vampires, the bogeyman, gremlins, and other monsters.

## NONFICTION

Darlene Trew Crist, *American Gargoyles: Spirits in Stone.* New York: Clarkson Potter, 2001. This book of photographs is the first one to depict the many gargoyles found throughout the United States. Photos are accompanied by stories and facts about gargoyles.

Jennifer Dussling, *Gargoyles: Monsters in Stone.* New York: Grosset & Dunlap, 1999. A brief historical guide to gargoyles, this book describes different kinds of gargoyles and how they are made.

Bo Zaunders and Roxie Munro, *Gargoyles, Girders, and Glass Houses: Magnificent Master Builders.* New York: Dutton Children's Books, 2004. This unique look at some of the world's most fascinating architectural structures introduces young readers to seven master builders, offers important scenes from their careers, and includes historical and architectural background on the structures they designed.

## WEB SITES

**Gargoyles and Cathedrals** (www.kn.pacbell. com/wired/fil/pages/listgargoyles.html). Created by middle school teacher Diane Adams, whose students were learning to sculpt gargoyles out of clay, this site contains many links to images of

gargoyles on cathedrals, historical information about gargoyles, and the Web sites of mod-
ern-day gargoyle carvers. The "Where am I?"
link takes students on a fun tour of New York's
gargoyles.

**Gargoyle Etymology and History** (www.
stratis.demon.co.uk/gargoyles/gg-ety-hist-
myth.htm). This easy-to-navigate site contains brief
information on the origins of gargoyles and their
architectural and religious history.

**Gargoyles and Grotesques: Carved in
Stone** (www.stonecarver.com/gargoyle.html).
Sculptor and stone carver Walter S. Arnold created
this site to describe the artistic process of carving
gargoyles, griffins, and chimeras in stone. The site
contains many professional photographs of
Arnold's work and includes some historical information about gargoyles.

**LCJ's Gargoyles Primer** (www.loonyarchi
vist.com/gargs). A good companion to the Gargoyles fan site below, this Web site provides
in-depth descriptions on the Gargoyles series characters and notes the episodes in which they have
played key roles.

**Station 8 Gargoyles Fan Site** (www.s8.org/
gargoyles). Fans of Disney's Gargoyles series can
browse this site to find links to ask series cocreator
Greg Weisman questions about the series and to
learn about the yearly Gargoyles convention.

# INDEX

# About the Author

Hayley Mitchell Haugen holds an MFA in poetry from the University of Washington, where she was awarded an Academy of American Poets Prize, and a PhD in American literature from Ohio University. She has taught creative writing, composition, and literature at various universities in Southern California and Ohio, and she has written numerous nonfiction books for teens and children published by Greenhaven Press, Lucent Books, and Kid-Haven Press.